DUDLEY SCHOOLS
LIBRARY SERVICE

KU-601-616

THIS WALKER BOOK BELONGS TO:

Schools Library and Information Services

S00000702272

DUDLEY PUBLIC LIBRARIES

L

702272 | | SCH

| JY KIG

First published 1987 by Walker Books Ltd
87 Vauxhall Walk, London SE11 5HJ

This edition published 1993

Reprinted 1993

© 1987 Rosalinda Kightley

Printed and bound in Hong Kong
by Sheck Wah Tong Printing Press Ltd

British Library Cataloguing in Publication Data
A catalogue record for this book is
available from the British Library.

ISBN 0-7445-3036-9

Busy Days

The Farmer

Rosalinda Kightley

WALKER BOOKS
LONDON

The farmer milks his cows at dawn,

Then he feeds the hens some corn.

The pigs get food

and fresh greens too,

The sheep are driven to pastures new.

Next the farmer bales the straw.

Then ploughs his fields

for an hour or more.

He picks ripe apples,

a bumper crop!

And digs up potatoes for the shop.

Then he clears the pond of weeds,

And gives the tractor the oil it needs.

At dusk he closes up the stable,

Then it's home for supper

at the kitchen table.

MORE WALKER PAPERBACKS
For You to Enjoy

TIME TO TALK
by Maureen Roffey

These lively and colourful books encourage young children to
talk about familiar objects and routines.

Mealtime   0-7445-2376-1
Bathtime   0-7445-2377-X
£2.99 each

THE POSTMAN
by Rosalinda Kightley

The postman's day is very busy. He cycles all round
town – from house to house, from the station to the school, from the
swimming pool to the supermarket – delivering letters and parcels. Simple
rhyming words and bright, bold pictures invite young children to
join the cheerful postman on his round.

0-7445-3035-0   £3.99

I SPY
by Maureen Roffey

On each page of these entertaining
observation game books there is something special
to spy – on the beach or at the zoo – and lots of fun for any young child.

I Spy at the Zoo   0-7445-2325-7
I Spy on Holiday   0-7445-2326-5
£2.99 each

**Walker Paperbacks are available from most booksellers, or by post from
Walker Books Ltd, PO Box 11, Falmouth, Cornwall TR10 9EN.**

To order, send: title, author, ISBN number and price for each book ordered, your full name and address
and a cheque or postal order for the total amount, plus postage and packing:

UK and BFPO Customers – £1.00 for first book, plus 50p for the second book and plus 30p for each additional book to a maximum charge of £3.00.
Overseas and Eire Customers – £2.00 for first book, plus £1.00 for the second book and plus 50p per copy for each additional book.
Prices are correct at time of going to press, but are subject to change without notice.